5-MINUTE GRATITUDE JOURNAL
FOR TEEN GIRLS

5-MINUTE GRATITUDE JOURNAL FOR TEEN GIRLS

Reflect, Give Thanks, and Find Joy

Charmaine Charmant

ROCKRIDGE
PRESS

For general information on our other products and services or to obtain technical support, please contact our Customer Care Department within the United States at (866) 744-2665, or outside the United States at (510) 253-0500.

Rockridge Press publishes its books in a variety of electronic and print formats. Some content that appears in print may not be available in electronic books, and vice versa.

TRADEMARKS: Rockridge Press and the Rockridge Press logo are trademarks or registered trademarks of Callisto Media Inc. and/or its affiliates, in the United States and other countries, and may not be used without written permission. All other trademarks are the property of their respective owners. Rockridge Press is not associated with any product or vendor mentioned in this book.

Interior and Cover Designer: Jill Lee
Art Producer: Hannah Dickerson
Editors: Erin Nelson and Maxine Marshall
Production Editor: Ruth Sakata Corley
Production Manager: Jose Olivera

All emojis used under license from Shutterstock.com

Author photo courtesy of Victoria Saperstein

Paperback ISBN: 978-1-63807-010-8
eBook ISBN: 978-1-63807-718-3
R0

For my sister
CHARNICE

"Gratitude opens the door, to the power, the wisdom, the creativity of the universe. You open the door through gratitude."

—DEEPAK CHOPRA

This journal belongs to: _____

You're in the Right Place

When was the last time that you felt a strong sense of appreciation for something or someone in your life? No matter how long that moment lasted, the feeling that you experienced is called gratitude. It's one word with big impact: Gratitude has the power to transform your life when you practice it daily.

My name is Charmaine Charmant, and I am excited to welcome you to this 5-minute gratitude journal made just for you. As a self-love author, my number one mission in life is to empower you to live happier and more confidently. How will you do this? The key lies in embracing your individuality.

Before you dive into the journal entries, I'm going to let you in on a little secret. The secret to falling in love with life is being intentional about setting a good tone for each and every day. It is incredible how writing your thoughts down on paper can ease your mind around the things that make you feel distracted and anxious.

For the longest time, I used to feel overwhelmed by school, social media, and constantly comparing myself to others. At first, I couldn't understand why I felt so unhappy all the time, but by taking five minutes to journal every day, I was able to shift my perspective and be more positive about all the things that were happening in my life. It's a wonderful feeling, and I am excited to pass this practice on to you, right here in these pages.

Why Gratitude Makes You Feel Better

Did you know that gratitude is associated with greater happiness? Psychology research from places like Harvard Medical School and *Forbes* magazine found that practicing gratitude made people healthier and encouraged positive thinking and stronger relationships.

Gratitude can also help you trust your instincts, feel more alive, and become more compassionate. By practicing gratitude through journaling, you can experience better sleep, a stronger immune system, lower blood pressure, increased resilience, and improved mental health. With this journal as your secret weapon, you are already on your way to feeling more calm, grateful, and happy with the world around you.

How to Use This Journal

This journal is a safe place for you to fully express yourself. There is no one you need to impress or perform for here—this is your private space, and you can be 100 percent free.

Here's a taste of what you can expect.

Empowering quotes. The quotes in this journal will remind you of why you are here, exploring this journey of gratitude. They will boost your self-esteem, help you banish negative thoughts, and allow you to thrive in the now.

Prompts for you. These prompts are meant to get you thinking about gratitude. Remember, there is no feeling of gratitude too small or too simple to write down. When answering the prompts, try to get as specific as possible.

"Get it, girl" affirmations. These affirmations will help you build the confidence and resilience needed to approach the world around you in a new way.

Pausing to reflect. Every 10 pages throughout the journal, there will be a page for you to pause and reflect on your experience with gratitude. Has your gratitude practice made an impact on your life? If so, how? Each Pause & Reflect will include a unique, attainable gratitude challenge.

While a daily gratitude practice is the fastest way to start feeling better, I want you to feel free to use this journal at any time or in any way that you please. These pages are for you and you alone. Go take what's yours.

What I Want to Get Out of This

At the end of this journal, I hope to feel _____

_____

_____

_____

By practicing gratitude, I will become _____

_____

_____

_____

I think journaling will make me feel more _____ and

less _____ because _____

Something I am struggling with is _____

_____

_____

_____

I believe gratitude can help because _____

_____

_____

_____

DATE:

_____ / _____ / _____

"Be thankful for what you have; you'll end up having more. If you concentrate on what you don't have, you will never, ever have enough."

—OPRAH WINFREY

Something I appreciate about myself is _____

_____

_____

Something that brings me joy is _____

_____

_____

Something a loved one has taught me is _____

_____

_____

A generous thing I did recently was _____

_____

_____

The only validation I need is from myself.

1

DATE:

_____ / _____ / _____

"The best thing is to realize that you are who you are and you gotta work with what you got."

—ZENDAYA

This week, I am looking forward to _____

_____

_____

Something I learned this year is _____

_____

_____

I am lucky to have _____

_____

_____

I am good at _____

_____

_____

I am doing what brings me joy.

DATE: ___ / ___ / ___

*"Gratitude is the healthiest of all human emotions.
The more you express gratitude for what you have, the more likely
you will have even more to express gratitude for."*

—ZIG ZIGLAR

Something that makes me proud is _____

_____

_____

Someone who I am lucky to have in my life is _____

_____

I really appreciated when _____

did _____

_____ for me.

My self-esteem is boosted when _____

_____

_____

Beauty comes in all forms. I am
beautiful—inside and out!

DATE:

_____ / _____ / _____

*"We can complain because rose bushes have thorns,
or rejoice because thorns have roses."*

—ALPHONSE KARR

Sometimes it's difficult to relate to my parents, but I love when they ___

_____

_____

Something that made me happy yesterday was _____

_____

_____

Gratitude can come in tiny units. Today I see it in _____

_____

_____

Something I often overlook but am blessed to have is _____

_____

_____

Every day, I see improvement, and I am grateful.

DATE:

_____ / _____ / _____

"We must find time to stop and thank the people who make
a difference in our lives."

—JOHN F. KENNEDY

The person who has had the biggest impact on my life is _____

_____

_____

I know I impacted _____ 's life when I _____

_____

_____

The person who I am most inspired by is _____

_____

_____

The last thing that I did for someone was _____

_____

_____

I will be the reason that someone smiles today.

DATE:

_____ / _____ / _____

"A grateful mind is a great mind which eventually attracts to itself great things."

—PLATO

This week I felt most confident when _____

_____

_____

One thing that makes me lucky is _____

_____

_____

Something I love about my body is _____

_____

_____

The best thing about my life right now is _____

_____

_____

I am brave and resilient.

DATE:

_____ / _____ / _____

*"Gratitude is a powerful catalyst for happiness.
It's the spark that lights a fire of joy in your soul."*
—AMY COLLETTE

I am looking forward to _____

_____

_____

Something I love about my life is _____

_____

_____

Something that went well today was _____

_____

_____

My favorite place in the world is _____

_____

_____

I have the confidence to be who I am, not
what the world expects me to be.

DATE:

_____ / _____ / _____

*"Appreciation is a wonderful thing. It makes what is
excellent in others belong to us as well."*

—VOLTAIRE

Today will be a great day because _____

_____

_____

Something I love about this month is _____

_____

_____

Someone who always makes me feel energized is _____

_____

_____

My favorite thing to do this time of year is _____

_____

_____

I am becoming more confident and comfortable
in my own skin every day.

DATE:

_____ / _____ / _____

"What separates privilege from entitlement is gratitude."

—BRENÉ BROWN

Today, I noticed _____ with new eyes.

A daily ritual that I love is _____

_____

_____

_____

The best part of my day today was _____

_____

_____

_____

I laugh the most when _____

_____

_____

_____

I already have everything that I need to succeed.

9

DATE:

_____ / _____ / _____

"No one is like you and that is your superpower."

—UNKNOWN

What makes me unique is _____

_____

_____

I am proud of my differences because _____

_____

_____

Someone who stands out and who I admire is _____

_____

_____

My superpower is my ability to _____

_____

_____

I accept myself entirely for who I am.

How am I feeling today?

_____

_____

With my gratitude practice, I've noticed _____

_____

_____

I never knew how grateful I could feel about _____

_____

_____

Gratitude Challenge

Do something unexpected for a friend today.

DATE:

_____ / _____ / _____

"Gratitude turns what we have into enough, and more."

—MELODY BEATTIE

My greatest strength lies in my _____

_____

_____

It's not always perfect, but something I like about school is _____

_____

_____

Something beautiful that I witnessed in school is _____

_____

_____

One way I like to move my body is _____

_____

_____

I accept and love myself exactly as I am. I am enough.

DATE:

_____ / _____ / _____

*"Enjoy the little things, for one day you may look back
and realize they were the big things."*

—ROBERT BRAULT

One activity that brings me joy is _____

_____

_____

I feel grateful for _____ when they _____

_____

_____

Something I take for granted but am really lucky to have is _____

_____

_____

I feel proud that I did _____

_____ for myself this week.

The universe is my oyster, and it supports me
in all the ways I need.

DATE:

_____ / _____ / _____

"Gratitude is the ability to experience life as a gift.
It liberates us from the prison of self-preoccupation."

—JOHN ORTBERG

A memory that brings me joy is _____

_____

_____

Something I love about the world is _____

_____

_____

I'd like to learn more about _____

_____

_____

A show that makes me feel happy is _____

_____

_____

There is no need to rush because what is
meant for me will never miss me.

DATE:

_____ / _____ / _____

"Feeling gratitude and not expressing it is like
wrapping a present and not giving it."

—WILLIAM ARTHUR WARD

I feel like the best version of myself when _____

_____

_____

I love my brain because _____

_____

_____

I feel most renewed when I _____

_____

_____

An outfit that makes me feel like my best self is _____

_____ because _____

_____

I am proud of my progress—I get better with time.

DATE:

_____ / _____ / _____

"... so many people had a hand in our success, from the teachers who inspired us to the janitors who kept our school clean ... and we were taught to value everyone's contribution and treat everyone with respect."

—MICHELLE OBAMA

An adult who inspires me is _____

_____

_____

Something I cherish is _____

_____

_____

I look up to _____ because they _____

_____

_____

I feel safest when _____

_____

_____

My life is full of positive energy. I am so
grateful to see another day.

DATE:

_____ / _____ / _____

"Enthusiasm is the electricity of life."

—GORDON PARKS

My life is amazing because of the following things: _____

_____

_____

I can look around the space that I am in and name three things that I

am grateful for: _____

_____

_____

One thing I used to feel self-conscious about but am now grateful for is

_____

_____

_____

I am grateful for my school because _____

_____

_____

I am rich in all areas of my life.

DATE:

_____ / _____ / _____

"When I started counting my blessings, my whole life turned around."

—WILLIE NELSON

My body takes care of me by _____

_____

_____

One thing I take for granted about my body is _____

_____

_____

I feel most confident when _____

_____

_____

My biggest fear seems irrelevant when _____

_____

_____

I breathe in confidence, and I exhale fear.

DATE:

_____ / _____ / _____

"Opening your eyes to more of the world around you can deeply enhance your gratitude practice."

—DERRICK CARPENTER

Something I am interested in learning more about is _____

_____

_____

The last time I felt curious was _____

_____

_____

I am happy that I changed my perspective on _____

_____

_____

I can see more of what the world has to offer by _____

_____

_____

Every day is a new opportunity
to put my best foot forward.

DATE: _____ / _____ / _____

"We often take for granted the very things that most deserve our gratitude."
—CYNTHIA OZICK

The last thing that I took for granted was _____

_____

_____

A luxury in life that I have is _____

_____

_____

This week, my friends made me feel happy by _____

_____

_____

Something I struggled with that made me stronger is _____

_____

_____

I do not worry about the future—I focus on
making the most of the present.

DATE:

_____ / _____ / _____

"When you are grateful, fear disappears and abundance appears."

—TONY ROBBINS

Nothing can stand in my way because _____

_____

_____

Some of my talents include _____

_____

_____

The last time I proved myself wrong was when _____

_____

_____

My wildest dream is _____

_____

_____

I am worthy of the things I desire.

How am I feeling today?

_____

_____

With my gratitude practice, I've noticed _____

_____

_____

A goal that my gratitude journal has inspired me to go after is _____

_____

_____

Gratitude Challenge

Think of someone in your life who you are grateful for and write a letter to them sharing how you feel.

DATE:

_____ / _____ / _____

"Be grateful for what you already have while you pursue your goals.
If you aren't grateful for what you already have, what makes you
think you would be happy with more?"

—ROY T. BENNETT

My favorite thing my body does is _____

_____

_____

An aspect of my life that I am happiest with is _____

_____

_____

Something beautiful that I get to see every day is _____

_____

_____

The sweetest thing that someone did for me recently was _____

_____

_____

I am blessed to have the life and body that I have.

DATE:

_____ / _____ / _____

"Eventually all things fall into place. Until then, laugh at the confusion,
live for the moments, and know everything happens for a reason."

—ALBERT SCHWEITZER

An experience that shaped me is _____

_____

_____

Something I used to dislike but now treasure is _____

_____

_____

A difficult experience that I overcame was _____

_____

_____

My family makes me better by _____

_____

_____

Everything that is happening now is
making me stronger.

DATE:

_____ / _____ / _____

"Gratitude makes sense of our past, brings peace for today,
and creates a vision for tomorrow."

—MELODY BEATTIE

Something from my past that I now understand is _____

_____

_____

Something I forgive myself for is _____

_____

_____

One thing that brings me peace today is _____

_____

_____

Something I want to do more of is _____

_____

_____

I show myself compassion because I deserve it.

DATE: _____ / _____ / _____

"Let us be grateful to the people who make us happy; they are the charming gardeners who make our souls blossom."

—MARCEL PROUST

I am happiest when I am with _____

_____

_____

Someone who always knows how to turn my frown upside down is ____

_____

_____

My biggest champion is _____

_____

_____

I honor my loved ones by _____

_____

_____

I add value to the lives of those around me.

26

DATE:

_____ / _____ / _____

"Gratitude is an antidote to negative emotions, a neutralizer of envy, hostility, worry, and irritation. It is savoring; it is not taking things for granted; it is present-oriented."

—SONJA LYUBOMIRSKY

I have an abundance of _____

_____

_____

The next time that I feel worried, I can calm myself by _____

_____

_____

Today I am grateful for _____

_____

_____

Dear me, the next time you feel sad, read this: _____

_____

_____

My life is beautiful and amazing. I don't need
to compare myself to others.

DATE:

_____ / _____ / _____

"I am convinced that life is 10% what happens to me and 90% how I react to it. And so it is with you ... We are in charge of our attitudes."

—CHARLES S. SWINDOLL

My favorite thing about nature is _____

_____

_____

My favorite time of day is _____

_____

_____

Something that makes my life easier is _____

_____

_____

I feel most innovative when _____

_____

_____

I choose to feel confident and amazing today.

DATE:

_____ / _____ / _____

*"Though I am grateful for the blessings of wealth, it hasn't changed who
I am. My feet are still on the ground. I just wear better shoes."*

—OPRAH WINFREY

Over the past couple of years, something I've grown to love is _____

_____

_____

I surprised myself when I _____

_____

_____

I found it really inspiring when _____

_____

_____

The last time that I felt empowered was _____

_____

_____

I am thankful I am learning and growing.

29

DATE:

_____ / _____ / _____

"The heart that gives thanks is a happy one,
for we cannot feel thankful and unhappy at the same time."

—DOUGLAS WOOD

My favorite vacation memory is _____

_____

_____

My favorite season is _____

_____

_____

My favorite neighborhood is _____

_____

_____

A place that makes me happy is _____

_____

_____

I appreciate my experiences for teaching me new things.

DATE:

_____ / _____ / _____

"Gratitude doesn't change the scenery. It merely washes clean the glass you look through so you can clearly see the colors."

—RICHELLE E. GOODRICH

The last time I saw a situation in a new light was _____

_____

_____

In this moment, three things I am grateful for are _____

_____

_____

I have grown in the last year by _____

_____

_____

I can appreciate the present more by _____

_____

_____

I am grateful to be alive.

DATE:

_____ / _____ / _____

"Everyone knows ice cream is worth the trouble of being cold."

—BRANDON SANDERSON

Something blocking me from unlocking my potential is _____

_____

I can change it by _____

_____

Someone who can help me face my fears is _____

_____

_____

I can ask _____ for support no matter what.

Being loved and supported makes me feel _____

_____

_____

I am not afraid to ask for help when I need it.

How am I feeling today?

_____

_____

With my gratitude practice, I've noticed _____

_____

_____

Something that surprised me this week was _____

_____

_____

Gratitude Challenge

Tell a family member something you value about them.

DATE:

_____ / _____ / _____

*"Today I choose to live with gratitude for the love that fills
my heart, the peace that rests within my spirit, and the voice
of hope that says all things are possible."*

—UNKNOWN

Something I worked hard to achieve is _____

_____

_____

I exhibited resilience when I _____

_____

_____

I surprised my community when I _____

_____

_____

I would describe my spirit as _____

_____

_____

I am learning every day.

DATE:

_____ / _____ / _____

"Gratitude is a way of opening the channel that will bring more, by contacting the true self and speaking from your heart."

—DEEPAK CHOPRA

The wisest person I know is _____

_____

_____

I feel most creative when _____

_____

_____

My power comes from _____

_____

_____

One thing I trust in is _____

_____

_____

I am resilient enough to reach the goals
I want to achieve.

DATE:

_____ / _____ / _____

"Gratitude helps you to grow and expand; gratitude brings joy and laughter into your life and into the lives of all those around you."

—EILEEN CADDY

Things that motivate me are _____

_____

_____

My top three goals for the day are _____

_____

_____

My favorite book is _____

_____

_____

Every day I look forward to _____

_____

_____

I invite gratitude into my heart.

DATE:

_____ / _____ / _____

"We can only be said to be alive in those moments
when our hearts are conscious of our treasure."

—THORTON WILDER

The air we breathe is so simple and yet so essential. I am grateful for it

because _____

_____

_____

Today, I woke up feeling _____

_____

_____

My perfect day looks like _____

_____

_____

I want to let go of _____

_____

_____

I am grateful to see another day.

DATE:

_____ / _____ / _____

"For once, stop and thank yourself for how far you've come. You've been trying to make changes in your life and all your efforts count."

—UNKNOWN

The last time I thanked myself was _____

_____

_____

I give myself credit for _____

_____

_____

Something special that I can plan for myself is _____

_____

_____

I have improved my life by _____

_____

_____

My life grows more beautiful with each day.

DATE:

_____ / _____ / _____

"I'm still thanking all the stars, one by one."

—MARISSA MEYER

Five years ago, I was _____

_____

_____

This year, I am _____

_____

_____

In 10 years, I will be _____

_____

_____

I am confident in my ability to get to where I want to be because _____

_____

_____

If I can dream it, it can happen—there's
nothing that is out of my reach.

DATE: _____ / _____ / _____

"Gratitude for the present moment and the fullness of life now is the true prosperity."

—ECKHART TOLLE

This moment is a good moment because _____

_____

_____

My most prized possession is _____

_____

_____

The things that make my life full are _____

_____

_____

The last time I did something for the first time was _____

_____

_____

I have so much to be grateful for,
and that makes life sweeter.

DATE:

_____ / _____ / _____

"Thankfulness is the quickest path to joy."

—JEFFERSON BETHKE

I feel the most joyful when _____

_____

_____

Today I am thankful for _____

_____

_____

Something I'm proud of that nobody knows about me is _____

_____

_____

I can make a positive difference today by _____

_____

_____

My thoughts have the power to influence my reality.

DATE:

_____ / _____ / _____

"When we focus on our gratitude, the tide of disappointment
goes out and the tide of love rushes in."

—KRISTIN ARMSTRONG

Someone who makes me feel safe is _____

_____

_____

A grudge that I want to let go of is _____

_____

_____

When I am stressed, I like to relax by _____

_____

_____

A fear that I want to conquer is _____

_____

_____

When I come back to my breath, I remember I can relax.

DATE:

_____ / _____ / _____

"When life is sweet, say thank you and celebrate. And when life is bitter, say thank you and grow."

—SHAUNA NIEQUIST

This week, my favorite moment at school was _____

_____

_____

What I learned from a difficult moment at school was _____

_____

_____

I am grateful for my bad experiences because _____

_____

_____

I like to celebrate myself by _____

_____

_____

I can get through anything because I am resilient.

43

PAUSE & REFLECT

How am I feeling today?

_____

_____

With my gratitude practice, I've noticed _____

_____

_____

Something that practicing gratitude helped me realize about myself is

_____

_____

_____

_____

Gratitude Challenge

Notice five beautiful things in nature today.

DATE:

_____ / _____ / _____

"Mindfulness isn't difficult, we just need to remember to do it."

—SHARON SALZBERG

The last time I felt 100 percent present was _____

_____

_____

I often daydream about _____

_____

_____

Something I want to limit so that I can be more present is _____

_____

_____

Somebody I've been meaning to thank is _____

_____

_____

I am always in the right place at the right time.

DATE:

_____ / _____ / _____

"When you practice gratefulness, there is a sense of respect towards others."

—DALAI LAMA

I feel most respected when _____

_____

_____

Three people who I deeply respect are _____

_____

_____

When I think about the world around me, I feel lucky to be me

because _____

_____

_____

Even on my hardest days, I have the luxury of _____

_____

_____

I respect myself and others.

DATE:

_____ / _____ / _____

"Within you, you will find everything you need to be complete."

—BRYANT MCGILL

I feel free when _____

_____

_____

Something it felt good to let go of was _____

_____

_____

By letting go of negative feelings, I hope to feel _____

_____

_____

I feel refreshed when _____

_____

_____

I accept the things I cannot change.

47

DATE:

_____ / _____ / _____

*"Acknowledging the good that you already have
in your life is the foundation for all abundance."*

—ECKHART TOLLE

When I give thanks, I feel _____

_____

_____

Something I forgot to give thanks for was _____

_____

_____

Right now, I am thankful that my body is allowing me to _____

_____

_____

I am thankful for my desires because they help me _____

_____

_____

I find happiness in the simple things
that life has to offer.

DATE:

_____ / _____ / _____

"Somewhere, something incredible is waiting to be known."

—SHARON BEGLEY

The last time that something incredible happened for me was _____

_____

_____

Something incredible that happened for my family was _____

_____

_____

I think my friends are incredible because _____

_____

_____

What makes me incredible is _____

_____

_____

Something incredible is about to happen for me.

DATE:

_____ / _____ / _____

"Identify your problems but give your power and energy to solutions."

—TONY ROBBINS

The last time I felt inspired by someone who overcame a problem was

_____

_____

_____

The last time I was faced with a problem, I made it through by _____

_____

_____

My energy is important because _____

_____

_____

When I focus on solutions instead of problems, I feel _____

_____

_____

There is always a path forward.

DATE:

_____ / _____ / _____

*"Small steps in the right direction can turn out
to be the biggest step of your life."*

—UNKNOWN

Something I did today to improve my future was _____

_____

_____

Something I did *last* week that impacted me in a positive way *this*

week was _____

_____

_____

Looking back, the best thing I ever did for myself was _____

_____

_____

Looking forward, the best thing I want to do for myself is _____

_____

_____

Good things are coming my way.

DATE:

_____ / _____ / _____

"The real gift of gratitude is that the more grateful you are,
the more present you become."

—ROBERT HOLDEN, PHD

I feel respected when _____

_____

_____

The last time I learned something new from someone unexpected was

_____

_____

What makes me unique from all my friends is _____

_____

_____

Thinking about my favorite teacher, what we have in common is _____

_____

_____ and what makes us different is

_____

I can disagree with others and still be worthy of respect.

DATE: _____ / _____ / _____

"Change the way you look at things and the things you look at change."

—WAYNE W. DYER

The last time I was amazed was when _____

_____

_____

_____ is a special person in my life. I love when they _____

_____

_____

A song that makes me feel happy is _____

_____

_____

The best thing I ate this week was _____

_____

_____

My feelings are valid, but they do not define me.
I am in control of my future!

53

DATE:

_____ / _____ / _____

"Now and then it's good to pause in our pursuit of happiness and just be happy."

—GUILLAUME APOLLINAIRE

One thing I value is _____

_____

_____

A new habit I want to adopt is _____

_____

_____

My favorite quote is _____

_____

_____

An artist I feel most inspired by is _____

_____

_____

I will never give up on myself or my dreams.

How am I feeling today?

_____

_____

With my gratitude practice, I've noticed _____

_____

_____

My gratitude practice has inspired me to _____

_____

_____

Gratitude Challenge

Make a list of five things you will do to honor yourself.

DATE:

_____ /_____ /_____

"It is very rare or almost impossible that an event can be negative from all points of view."

—DALAI LAMA

What detail of your day brings you the most joy? _____

_____

_____

What detail of your day can you bring more attention to? _____

_____

_____

How can you be more present in your day-to-day life? _____

_____

_____

What are some things that you may not be noticing throughout your

routine that could make your day a little bit brighter? _____

_____

_____

My life is full of beauty and wonder.

DATE:

_____ / _____ / _____

"A smile is a curve that sets everything straight."

—PHYLLIS DILLER

What are some things that bring a smile to your face? _____

_____

_____

Reflect on how you feel when you smile. _____

_____

_____

When was the last time you made someone else smile? _____

_____

_____

What would inspire you to smile more on a daily basis? _____

_____

_____

My smile has the power to improve my day.

DATE:

_____ / _____ / _____

"Some days there won't be a song in your heart. Sing anyway."

—EMORY AUSTIN

How do you cheer yourself up when you're feeling sad? _____

_____

_____

Reflect on a time when there wasn't a song in your heart but you sang

anyway. What did you learn from that experience? _____

_____

_____

In whom can you confide when you're not having a good day? _____

_____

_____

Can a bad day create positive results? _____

_____

_____

My life is amazing, even on the days
when it feels like it isn't.

*"Joy is what happens to us when we allow ourselves
to recognize how good things really are."*

—MARIANNE WILLIAMSON

What is something that you would miss if it were taken away? _____

_____

_____

_____

Is there something in your life that you often take for granted? _____

_____

_____

What is something that makes your life unique? _____

_____

_____

What are some things that others struggle with that you don't have to?

_____

_____

I am lucky to have such a rich and fulfilling life.

DATE:

_____ / _____ / _____

"Things are beautiful if you love them."

—JEAN ANOUILH

What does beauty mean to you? _____

_____

_____

What makes you feel most beautiful? _____

_____

_____

What things in your life do you overlook? What is beautiful about them?

_____

_____

_____

What are three personality traits that make you beautiful? _____

_____

_____

My beauty is evolving and never-ending.

DATE: _____ / _____ / _____

"All our dreams can come true, if we have the courage to pursue them."

—WALT DISNEY

Today I woke up and thought _____

_____

_____

My biggest dream is to _____

_____

_____

I am actively working on achieving my dream by _____

_____

_____

Every day, I work on reaching my goal by _____

_____

_____

I believe I can do anything.

DATE:

_____ / _____ / _____

*"To me, beauty is about being comfortable in your own skin.
It's about knowing and accepting who you are."*

—ELLEN DEGENERES

How would you describe yourself to a stranger? _____

_____

_____

When do you feel most comfortable in your own skin? _____

_____

_____

What are the things that you haven't accepted about yourself? How

can you work on accepting them? _____

_____

_____

What makes you grateful to be you? _____

_____

_____

I am proud of who I am and the skin that I am in.

DATE:

_____ / _____ / _____

"If you have good thoughts they will shine out of your face like sunbeams."

—ROALD DAHL

Do your thoughts influence the way you feel? Why or why not? _____

_____

_____

_____

Reflect on the last time a happy thought put you in a great mood. _____

_____

_____

Think back to your happiest moment. Describe it. _____

_____

_____

Reflect on a time when you laughed uncontrollably. _____

_____

_____

My thoughts are a powerful tool that I can use to
experience joy.

"I wish I'd known that I already had everything I needed within myself to be happy, instead of looking for happiness at beauty counters."

—ILENE BECKERMAN

What makes you happy to be you? _____

_____

_____

What are your best qualities? _____

_____

_____

When was the last time you impressed yourself? _____

_____

_____

Reflect on a time when you displayed resilience. _____

_____

_____

I have everything I need to live my best life.

DATE:

_____ / _____ / _____

*"... some days you might be overwhelmingly sad, or some days you might
be very angry. Some days you might be really happy, and all of these
feelings are real, and they're legitimate, and they're yours.... You don't
[need to] feel like you need to hide them or you need to push them away,
because they're your feelings and you are an incredible person, you're
a sensitive person, and there's space for them."*

—TROIAN BELLISARIO

I feel most in touch with my emotions when _____

_____

_____

I appreciate my feelings because they _____

_____

When I try to hide my feelings, it makes me _____

_____

I am not ashamed of my feelings because _____

_____

_____

My feelings are natural. They are here to support me
through my life journey.

PAUSE & REFLECT

How am I feeling today?

_____

_____

With my gratitude practice, I've noticed _____

_____

_____

A blessing that I am grateful for is _____

_____

_____

Gratitude Challenge

Sign up for a new activity that you've been too scared to try.

DATE:

_____ / _____ / _____

"It is amazing how a little tomorrow can make up for a whole lot of yesterday."

—JOHN GUARE

I am in love with myself because _____

_____

_____

I am in love with my friends because _____

_____

_____

I am in love with my family because _____

_____

_____

I am in love with life because _____

_____

_____

My life is bountiful! I am curious about everything that is in store for me.

DATE: _____ / _____ / _____

"Focusing on one thing that you are grateful for increases the energy of gratitude and rises the joy inside yourself."

—OPRAH WINFREY

The most unpredictable thing that happened to me was _____

_____

_____

The best surprise I ever received was _____

_____

_____

When the future is uncertain, I feel _____

_____

_____

I am not afraid of the unknown because _____

_____

_____

I embrace the unknown because I can handle
anything that life throws my way.

DATE:

_____ / _____ / _____

"Write it on your heart that every day is the best day in the year."
—RALPH WALDO EMERSON

I am passionate about _____

_____

_____

My personal style can be described as _____

_____

_____

I feel compassion for _____

_____

_____

I feel humbled by _____

_____

_____

I can chase and fulfill my desires.

DATE:

_____ / _____ / _____

*"The more you praise and celebrate your life, the more
there is in life to celebrate."*

—OPRAH WINFREY

The last thing I celebrated was _____

_____

_____

I am looking forward to celebrating _____

_____

_____

Something that I would like to celebrate more is _____

_____

_____

Someone or something in my life that I praise is _____

_____

_____

My life is incredible and worth celebrating.

DATE:

_____ / _____ / _____

"We can let the circumstances of our lives harden us ... or we can let them soften us, and make us kinder. You always have the choice."

—DALAI LAMA

I feel most alive when _____

_____

_____

Something good that happened to me recently was _____

_____

_____

Something bad that happened to me recently was _____

_____

_____

My experiences teach me that _____

_____

_____

I have a life full of adventures.

DATE:

_____ / _____ / _____

"Follow your bliss. Find where it is, and don't be afraid to follow it."

—JOSEPH CAMPBELL

The last time I felt like I hit a wall was _____

_____

_____

Feeling stuck has taught me that _____

_____

_____

The last time a major opportunity opened up for me was _____

_____

_____

Following my bliss means _____

_____

_____

A roadblock is a place where I just haven't
found a solution *yet.*

DATE:

_____ / _____ / _____

"The world needs that special gift that only you have."

—MARIE FORLEO

What makes me special is _____

_____

_____

I make an impact in my community by _____

_____

_____

A skill that I plan to cultivate is _____

_____

_____

Something I look forward to learning is _____

_____

_____

The world benefits from having me in it.

DATE:

_____ / _____ / _____

"Think about it: What's the worst thing that can happen
to you if you just totally go for it?"

—GRANT CARDONE

Something I went for and didn't get was _____

_____

_____

Something I want to try is _____

_____

_____

I am in the best position to chase my dreams because _____

_____

_____

Something I learned from failing was _____

_____

_____

I am capable of achieving my wildest dreams.

74

"I find that life can become so complex that we can forget the things in life that were meant to bring us the most pleasure."

—DOLORES AYOTTE

Sometimes I feel overwhelmed by _____

_____

_____

Something that helps me feel less overwhelmed is _____

_____

_____

I am at peace when I am _____

_____

_____

Something that will bring me joy today is _____

_____

_____

I know that uneasy feelings are temporary and will pass.

DATE:

_____ / _____ / _____

"To live a full life is to live one without regrets."

—REBECCA K. SAMPSON

Something I wish I took advantage of is _____

_____

_____

One way I plan on having fewer regrets is by _____

_____

_____

My life feels full when _____

_____

_____

My best life looks like _____

_____

_____

As long as I am living and learning,
I will have no regrets.

76

How am I feeling today?

_____

_____

With my gratitude practice, I've noticed _____

_____

_____

The content I consume on social media makes me feel _____.

_____

_____

Gratitude Challenge

Go to your favorite social media platform and unfollow people
that make you feel unhappy.

DATE:

_____ / _____ / _____

"I'm looking forward to continuing to learn from my past, living in the present, and surrendering to the future."

—BEYONCÉ

I am looking forward to _____

_____

_____

My past taught me that _____

_____

_____

I love living in the present because _____

_____

_____

The future excites me because _____

_____

_____

My life is full of lessons that will
make me a better person.

DATE:

_____ / _____ / _____

"Just around the bend, a miracle is waiting to happen. Release fear and uncertainty, and majestic wonders wait to unfold for you."

—DENISE LINN

Something miraculous that happened to me is _____

_____

_____

I combat fear by _____

_____

_____

When I let go of my fears, I feel _____

_____

_____

One way I navigate uncertainty is to _____

_____

_____

Amazing things surprise me every day.

DATE:

_____ / _____ / _____

"The strongest light is the light that shines within you.
Use it to lead the way of your life."

—UNKNOWN

I shine brightly because _____

_____

_____

A positive trait that my loved ones passed on to me is _____

_____

_____

I am grateful for my perspective on _____

_____

_____

Something nonphysical that makes me stand out is _____

_____

_____

I am magnetic, and nothing can stand
in the way of my greatness.

DATE:

_____ / _____ / _____

"The purpose of life, after all, is to live it, to taste experience to the utmost, to reach out eagerly and without fear for newer and richer experience."

—ELEANOR ROOSEVELT

The last time I felt like I was living life to the fullest was _____

_____

_____

The last time I experienced growth from an experience was _____

_____

_____

I feel rich when _____

_____

_____

New experiences make me feel _____

_____

_____

I will have many rich experiences throughout
the course of my life.

DATE:

_____ / _____ / _____

"Every day, it's important to ask and answer these questions: 'What's good in my life?' and 'What needs to be done?'"

—NATHANIEL BRANDEN

Something good in my life is _____

_____

_____

Something inspiring in my life is _____

_____

_____

Something I want to work on is _____

_____

_____

Something I look forward to accomplishing is _____

_____

_____

I have an infinite number of things to be grateful for.

DATE:

_____ / _____ / _____

"There is no greater gift you can give or receive than to honor your calling.
It's why you were born. And how you become most truly alive."

—OPRAH WINFREY

I feel like my life's calling is _____

_____

_____

I am naturally gifted with _____

_____

_____

I feel most purposeful when _____

_____

_____

I am most at ease when I am _____

_____

_____

I am on the right path and walking in my purpose.

DATE:

_____ / _____ / _____

"Don't be pushed by your problems. Be led by your dreams."

—RALPH WALDO EMERSON

A time when I solved a difficult problem was when _____

_____

_____

When I view my problems as learning opportunities, I feel _____

_____

_____

I believe in my dreams because _____

_____

_____

In 10 years, I will be _____

_____

_____

My dreams will become my reality.

DATE:

_____ / _____ / _____

"Whatever the mind can conceive and believe, it can achieve."

—NAPOLEON HILL

When I have no worries, my body feels _____

_____

_____

Something that helps me forget about my worries is _____

_____

_____

Things will work out for me because _____

_____

_____

I cope with worry by _____

_____

_____

There are no wrong paths, only lessons.

DATE:

_____ / _____ / _____

"The power of positive thinking is the ability to generate a feeling of certainty in yourself when nothing in the environment supports you."

—TONY ROBBINS

No matter what is going on around me, I will be okay because _____

_____

_____

A time when I thrived in an uncertain environment was _____

_____

_____

When I think positively, I notice _____

_____

_____

My most positive friend is _____ . One thing I would like to

model after them is _____

_____

I will succeed no matter what life throws my way.

DATE:

_____ / _____ / _____

"My mission in life is not merely to survive, but to thrive."

—MAYA ANGELOU

To me, surviving means _____

_____

_____

Something I survived was _____

_____

_____

To me, thriving means _____

_____

_____

I thrive when _____

_____

_____

I am always thriving and living my best life.

87

How am I feeling today?

_____

_____

With my gratitude practice, I've noticed _____

_____

_____

My experiences at school make me feel _____

_____

_____

Gratitude Challenge

Ask three people what they are grateful for today.

DATE:

_____ / _____ / _____

"The root of joy is gratefulness . . . It is not joy that makes us grateful; it is gratitude that makes us joyful."

—BROTHER DAVID STEINDL-RAST

One thing I am happy about in this moment is _____

_____

_____

I am grateful for this present moment because _____

_____

_____

When I push things off, it makes me feel _____

_____

_____

When I focus on the present, _____

_____

_____

I am building the life of my dreams every day.

DATE:

_____ / _____ / _____

"You do not find the happy life. You make it."

—CAMILLA EYRING KIMBALL

I make myself happy by _____

_____

_____

I make others happy by _____

_____

_____

Something I did that amazes me is _____

_____

_____

Every day, I become happier by _____

_____

_____

I make happiness wherever I go.

"Do not spoil what you have by desiring what you have not; remember that what you now have was once among the things you only hoped for."

—EPICURUS

Something I accomplished that I never thought I could is _____

_____

_____

Something I used to want that I now have is _____

_____

_____

Something I learned that used to be a mystery to me is _____

_____

_____

Someone that recently came into my life that I am grateful for is _____

_____

_____

My life is abundant!

DATE:

_____ / _____ / _____

*"At all times and under all circumstances, we have
the power to transform the quality of our lives."*

—WERNER ERHARD

The last time that something unexpected happened to me was _____

_____

_____

A connection I would like to build on is _____

_____

_____

It is never too late to _____

_____

_____

I feel most powerful when _____

_____

_____

It's never too late to build a better tomorrow.

DATE:

_____ / _____ / _____

"A loving heart is the beginning of all knowledge."

—THOMAS CARLYLE

Someone I hold close to my heart is _____

_____

_____

An experience I hold close to my heart is _____

_____

_____

I know that I have a lot of love in my heart because _____

_____

_____

I can open up my heart to others by _____

_____

_____

I am a loving person who will receive 10 times more
than what I put into the world.

DATE:

_____ / _____ / _____

"Never regret anything that made you smile."

—MARK TWAIN

Some good news I recently received was _____

_____

_____

A recent accomplishment of mine is _____

_____

_____

I know that my potential is endless because _____

_____

_____

In my life, I aspire to _____

_____

_____

I can accomplish anything that I set my mind to.

DATE:

_____ / _____ / _____

*"We have within us an extraordinary capacity
for love, joy, and unshakable freedom."*

—JACK KORNFIELD

To me, loving life means _____

_____

_____

Something that makes my life better is _____

_____

_____

The greatest example of love that I've witnessed is _____

_____

_____

Life loves me back by _____

_____

_____

My life is beautiful and full of love.

DATE:

_____ / _____ / _____

"What good is warmth without cold to give it sweetness?"

—JOHN STEINBECK

Some things in my life I can't control are _____

_____

_____

Letting go of things I can't control makes me feel _____

_____

_____

I want my life to be _____

_____

_____

I commit to leading with _____

_____

_____

I live life with a positive outlook.

DATE:

_____ / _____ / _____

"Start each day with a grateful heart."

—UNKNOWN

I woke up today and felt _____

_____

_____

I woke up today and saw _____

_____

_____

I woke up today and touched _____

_____

_____

I woke up today knowing that _____

_____

_____

Each day is a gift and a testament to my worthiness.

DATE: _____ / _____ / _____

"Accept what life offers you and try to drink from every cup."

—PAULO COELHO

A life with no regrets looks like _____

_____

_____

Living my best life means _____

_____

_____

I enjoy things the most when _____

_____

_____

I can make the most out of life by simply _____

_____

_____

I have the power to design the life of my dreams.

How am I feeling today?

_____

_____

With my gratitude practice, I've noticed _____

_____

_____

How have I grown since starting to use this journal? _____

_____

_____

Gratitude Challenge

Do something out of your comfort zone today.

DATE:

_____ / _____ / _____

"If you worry about what might be and wonder what might have been, you will ignore what is."

—UNKNOWN

Something I am currently taking for granted is _____

_____

_____

Something I wish I didn't waste time worrying about is _____

_____

_____

I worry less when _____

_____

_____

I truly appreciate the present when _____

_____

_____

No time is more important than the present moment—here and now.

DATE:

_____ / _____ / _____

"The greatest self is a peaceful smile, that always
sees the world smiling back."

—BRYANT MCGILL AND JENNI YOUNG

What does beauty mean to you? _____

_____

_____

The most beautiful thing I've ever witnessed is _____

_____

_____

Today I smiled because _____

_____

_____

Things that make me smile on a daily basis are _____

_____

_____

Life is not perfect, and that is what makes it beautiful.

DATE: _____ / _____ / _____

"Do not let what you cannot do interfere with what you can do."

—JOHN WOODEN

Some internal beliefs that limit me from achieving my goals are _____

_____

_____

When my limiting beliefs interfere with what I set out to do, it makes

me feel _____

_____

_____

Two ways to get over my limiting beliefs are _____

_____

_____

Someone I can talk to about pushing past my fears is _____

_____

_____

I am nurturing my passions and cultivating my talent.

DATE:

_____ / _____ / _____

"We just need to be kinder to ourselves. If we treated ourselves the way we treated our best friend, can you imagine how much better off we would be?"

—MEGHAN MARKLE

I tend to focus on what others are doing when _____

_____

_____

Comparing my journey to others' makes me feel _____

_____

_____

My journey is unique in the following ways: _____

_____

_____

Comparing myself to others isn't productive because _____

_____

_____

I am confident because I know my strength.

"Love the moment. Flowers grow out of dark moments.
Therefore, each moment is vital. It affects the whole. Life is a
succession of such moments and to live each is to succeed."

—CORITA KENT

To me, truly loving a moment means _____

_____

_____

One thing I love about this moment is _____

_____

_____

A dark moment that taught me a lot was _____

_____

_____

A routine moment that is important to my well-being is _____

_____

_____

I commit to making the best of each moment
that life gifts me with.

DATE:

_____ / _____ / _____

"We should remember that just as a positive outlook on life can promote good health, so can everyday acts of kindness."

—HILLARY CLINTON

An act of kindness I recently witnessed was _____

_____

_____

The last kind thing I did was _____

_____

_____

When someone is kind to me, I feel _____

_____

_____

When I think about the kindest person in my life, I feel most inspired

by their _____

_____

_____

I lead with kindness, and the world loves me for it.

DATE:

_____ / _____ / _____

"Often we imagine that we will work hard until we arrive at some distant goal, and then we will be happy. This is a delusion. Happiness is the result of a life lived with purpose. Happiness is not an objective. It is the movement of life itself, a process, and an activity."

—ETHAN HAWKE

A distant goal that will bring me happiness is _____

_____

_____

I can enjoy the process of reaching that goal by _____

_____

_____

Three different ways I've experienced happiness are _____

_____

_____

I can work on finding my purpose by _____

_____

_____

I choose to pursue peace and happiness every day.

*"There's beauty in the things we think are imperfect.
That sounds very cliché, but it's true."*

—LAVERNE COX

What three things make you perfectly imperfect? _____

_____

_____

How can you view imperfections in your life in a positive light? _____

_____

_____

Nobody's perfect. Think about your favorite celebrity or role model.

What are some of their imperfections? _____

_____

_____

What are some nontraditional things that you love? _____

_____

_____

My imperfections are incredible, and they bring me joy.

DATE:

_____ / _____ / _____

"Don't let the noise of others' opinions drown your own inner voice. And most important, have the courage to follow your heart and intuition. They somehow already know what you truly want to become."

—STEVE JOBS

I can make time to listen to my inner voice by _____

_____

_____

Something I want to explore for me is _____

_____

_____

Something I do simply because others are doing it is _____

_____

_____

My unique purpose in life is _____

_____

_____

I am confident enough to forge my own path in life.

DATE:

_____ / _____ / _____

"Instead of complaining about your circumstances,
get busy and create some new ones."

—RALPH MARSTON

The last time I complained about my circumstances was _____

_____

_____

I can shift the way I view my circumstances by _____

_____

_____

I can create new circumstances by _____

_____

_____

I can keep myself busy with _____

_____

_____

Nothing in life has to remain the same. I can have
whatever my heart desires.

How am I feeling today?

_____

_____

With my gratitude practice, I've noticed _____

_____

_____

I realize that I am really good at _____

_____

_____

Gratitude Challenge

Share a positive affirmation with a friend today.

DATE:

_____ / _____ / _____

"In the middle of every difficulty lies opportunity."

—ALBERT EINSTEIN

When things get difficult, I feel _____

_____

_____

For me, taking a step back when things get hard looks like _____

_____

_____

When a new opportunity comes along, I feel _____

_____

_____

Ways that I can start to look at problems as opportunities instead of

setbacks are by _____

_____

_____

The more challenges I face, the stronger I become.

DATE:

_____ / _____ / _____

"The clouds above us join and separate, The breeze in the courtyard leaves and returns. Life is like that, so why not relax? Who can stop us from celebrating?"

—LU YU

I love celebrations because _____

_____

_____

I celebrate life by _____

_____

_____

I praise myself by _____

_____

_____

I praise others by _____

_____

_____

I am full of joy and love.

DATE:

_____ / _____ / _____

"Life isn't about waiting for the storm to pass ... It's about learning to dance in the rain!"

—VIVIAN GREENE

The last time I made the best of a situation was _____

_____

_____

I feel unstoppable when _____

_____

_____

It is easy for me to change my perspective on things when _____

_____

_____

Hard times can teach us _____

_____

_____

Life is easy for me because I can always substitute
a positive thought for a negative one.

DATE:

_____ / _____ / _____

"And so each venture is a new beginning."

—T. S. ELIOT

To me, a fresh beginning means _____

_____

_____

Today is a fresh beginning, and I will use it to _____

_____

_____

Internally, I can create fresh beginnings by _____

_____

_____

In my relationships, I can cultivate fresh beginnings by _____

_____

_____

Today will be my happiest day.

DATE:

_____ / _____ / _____

"Happiness [is] only real when shared."

—CHRIS MCCANDLESS

A compliment I always receive is _____

_____

_____

My biggest admirer has mentioned _____

_____

_____

My greatest strength is _____

_____

_____

When I am feeling down, I can count on _____

_____

_____

I am greater than I could ever imagine.

DATE: _____ / _____ / _____

"Happiness is like a butterfly; the more you chase it, the more it will elude you, but if you turn your attention to other things, it will come and sit softly on your shoulder."

—UNKNOWN

I feel least happy when _____

_____

_____

I can eliminate things that don't make me happy by _____

_____

_____

I pay close attention to _____

_____

_____

I enjoy spending my time _____

_____

_____

I accept the things I cannot change and love life anyway.

DATE:

_____ / _____ / _____

"I'm in no hurry; the sun and the moon aren't either."

—FERNANDO PESSOA AS ALBERTO CAEIRO

When I am in a hurry, I feel _____

_____

_____

When I take my time, I feel _____

_____

_____

When something no longer makes sense, I _____

_____

_____

Pursuing something in which I am genuinely interested makes me feel

_____

_____

_____

I live my life for myself, not for others.

DATE:

_____ / _____ / _____

*"If you want to be proud of yourself, then do
things in which you can take pride."*

—KAREN HORNEY

Three words that best describe me and why are _____

_____

_____

Three things I love about myself today are _____

_____

_____

My most redeeming quality is _____

_____

_____

What I want the most out of life is _____

_____

_____

I love myself for who I am unconditionally.

DATE:

_____ / _____ / _____

"Nothing is more honorable than a grateful heart."

— LUCIUS ANNAEUS SENECA

Think of someone you know who has a grateful heart. What do you admire about this person? _____

_____

_____

What are you currently grateful for? _____

_____

_____

When was the last time that you expressed gratitude to someone in your life? _____

_____

_____

Reflect on the things that you are grateful for. _____

_____

_____

Good things are always coming my way.

DATE:

_____ / _____ / _____

"Today I choose life. Every morning when I wake up I can choose joy, happiness, negativity, pain ... today I choose to feel life, not to deny my humanity but embrace it."

—KEVYN AUCOIN

Where are you on your journey of self-acceptance? _____

_____

_____

How can you work on accepting the things you cannot change? _____

_____

_____

What do you enjoy about your life right now? _____

_____

_____

What are some things that you don't want to miss out on? _____

_____

_____

I am exactly where the universe needs me to be.

What I Got Out of This

Through journaling, I achieved my goal of _____

_____

_____

I used to think gratitude was about _____

_____

_____

Now I understand gratitude means _____

_____

_____

My outlook about _____ has changed because

_____

_____

The biggest lesson that this journal has taught me is _____

_____

_____

About the Author

Charmaine Charmant is a New York City native of Caribbean descent with a passion for women's empowerment and fashion. She earned her B.A. from Wellesley College and her M.S. in Management from Wake Forest University prior to becoming a fashion and lifestyle content creator. Her work, which encourages women to embrace their individuality and live confidently in style, has been featured on ABC 7, xoNecole, and Buzzfeed. To learn more about Charmaine, visit CharmaineCharmant.com.

CPSIA information can be obtained
at www.ICGtesting.com
Printed in the USA
JSHW032354141021
19559JS00006B/47